Instructional Guide for Literature

D0864610

Last Stop on Market Street

A guide for the book by Matt de la Peña
Great Works author: Jodene Lynn Smith, M.A.

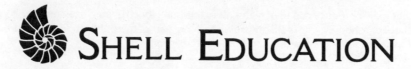

SHELL EDUCATION

Publishing Credits

Corinne Burton, M.A.Ed., *President*; Emily R. Smith, M.A.Ed., *Content Director*; Lee Aucoin, *Multimedia Designer*; Stephanie Bernard, *Assistant Editor*; Don Tran, *Graphic Designer*

Image Credits

iStock (cover)

Standards

© 2007 Teachers of English to Speakers of Other Languages, Inc. (TESOL)
© 2007 Board of Regents of the University of Wisconsin System. World-Class Instructional Design and Assessment (WIDA)
© Copyright 2010. National Governors Association Center for Best Practices and Council of Chief State School Officers. All rights reserved.

Shell Education

a division of Teacher Created Materials
5301 Oceanus Drive
Huntington Beach, CA 92649-1030
ISBN 978-1-4258-1647-6
https://www.tcmpub.com/shell-education
© 2017 Shell Educational Publishing, Inc.

Table of contents

How to Use This Literature Guide

Today's standards demand rigor and relevance in the reading of complex texts. The units in this series guide teachers in a rich and deep exploration of worthwhile works of literature for classroom study. The most rigorous instruction can also be interesting and engaging!

Many current strategies for effective literacy instruction have been incorporated into these instructional guides for literature. Throughout the units, text-dependent questions are used to determine comprehension of the book as well as student interpretation of the vocabulary words. The books chosen for the series are complex and are exemplars of carefully crafted works of literature. Close reading is used throughout the units to guide students toward revisiting the text and using textual evidence to respond to prompts orally and in writing. Students must analyze the story elements in multiple assignments for each section of the book. All of these strategies work together to rigorously guide students through their study of literature.

The next few pages describe how to use this guide for a purposeful and meaningful literature study. Each section of this guide is set up in the same way to make it easier for you to implement the instruction in your classroom.

Theme Thoughts

The great works of literature used throughout this series have important themes that have been relevant to people for many years. Many of the themes will be discussed during the various sections of this instructional guide. However, it would also benefit students to have independent time to think about the key themes of the book.

Before students begin reading, have them complete the *Pre-Reading Theme Thoughts* (page 13). This graphic organizer will allow students to think about the themes outside the context of the story. They'll have the opportunity to evaluate statements based on important themes and defend their opinions. Be sure to keep students' papers for comparison to the *Post-Reading Theme Thoughts* (page 59). This graphic organizer is similar to the pre-reading activity. However, this time, students will be answering the questions from the point of view of one of the characters in the book. They have to think about how the character would feel about each statement and defend their thoughts. To conclude the activity, have students compare what they thought about the themes before they read the book to what the characters discovered during the story.

How to Use This Literature Guide (cont.)

Vocabulary

Each teacher reference vocabulary overview page has definitions and sentences about how key vocabulary words are used in the section. These words should be introduced and discussed with students. Students will use these words in different activities throughout the book.

On some of the vocabulary student pages, students are asked to answer text-related questions about vocabulary words from the sections. The following question stems will help you create your own vocabulary questions if you'd like to extend the discussion.

- How does this word describe _____'s character?
- How does this word connect to the problem in this story?
- How does this word help you understand the setting?
- Tell me how this word connects to the main idea of this story.
- What visual pictures does this word bring to your mind?
- Why do you think the author used this word?

At times, you may find that more work with the words will help students understand their meanings and importance. These quick vocabulary activities are a good way to further study the words.

- Students can play vocabulary concentration. Make one set of cards that has the words on them and another set with the definitions. Then, have students lay them out on the table and play concentration. The goal of the game is to match vocabulary words with their definitions. For early readers or English language learners, the two sets of cards could be the words and pictures of the words.

- Students can create word journal entries about the words. Students choose words they think are important and then describe why they think each word is important within the book. Early readers or English language learners could instead draw pictures about the words in a journal.

- Students can create puppets and use them to act out the vocabulary words from the stories. Students may also enjoy telling their own character-driven stories using vocabulary words from the original stories.

How to Use This Literature Guide (cont.)

Analyzing the Literature

After you have read each section with students, hold a small-group or whole-class discussion. Provided on the teacher reference page for each section are leveled questions. The questions are written at two levels of complexity to allow you to decide which questions best meet the needs of your students. The Level 1 questions are typically less abstract than the Level 2 questions. These questions are focused on the various story elements, such as character, setting, and plot. Be sure to add further questions as your students discuss what they've read. For each question, a few key points are provided for your reference as you discuss the book with students.

Reader Response

In today's classrooms, there are often great readers who are below average writers. So much time and energy is spent in classrooms getting students to read on grade level that little time is left to focus on writing skills. To help teachers include more writing in their daily literacy instruction, each section of this guide has a literature-based reader response prompt. Each of the three genres of writing is used in the reader responses within this guide: narrative, informative/explanatory, and opinion. Before students write, you may want to allow them time to draw pictures related to the topic. Book-themed writing paper is provided on page 69 if your students need more space to write.

Guided Close Reading

Within each section of this guide, it is suggested that you closely reread a portion of the text with your students. The sections to be reread are described by location within the story since there are no page numbers in these books. After rereading the section, there are a few text-dependent questions to be answered by students.

Working space has been provided to help students prepare for the group discussion. They should record their thoughts and ideas on the activity page and refer to it during your discussion. Rather than just taking notes, you may want to require students to write complete responses to the questions before discussing them with you.

Encourage students to read one question at a time and then go back to the text and discover the answer. Work with students to ensure that they use the text to determine their answers rather than making unsupported inferences. Suggested answers are provided in the answer key.

How to Use This Literature Guide (cont.)

Guided Close Reading (cont.)

The generic open-ended stems below can be used to write your own text-dependent questions if you would like to give students more practice.

- What words in the story support . . . ?
- What text helps you understand . . . ?
- Use the book to tell why _____ happens.
- Based on the events in the story, . . . ?
- Show me the part in the text that supports . . . .
- Use the text to tell why . . . .

Making Connections

The activities in this section help students make cross-curricular connections to mathematics, science, social studies, fine arts, or other curricular areas. These activities require higher-order thinking skills from students but also allow for creative thinking.

Language Learning

A special section has been set aside to connect the literature to language conventions. Through these activities, students will have opportunities to practice the conventions of standard English grammar, usage, capitalization, and punctuation.

Story Elements

It is important to spend time discussing what the common story elements are in literature. Understanding the characters, setting, plot, and theme can increase students' comprehension and appreciation of the story. If teachers begin discussing these elements in early childhood, students will more likely internalize the concepts and look for the elements in their independent reading. Another very important reason for focusing on the story elements is that students will be better writers if they think about how the stories they read are constructed.

In the story elements activities, students are asked to create work related to the characters, setting, or plot. Consider having students complete only one of these activities. If you give students a choice on this assignment, each student can decide to complete the activity that most appeals to him or her. Different intelligences are used so that the activities are diverse and interesting to all students.

How to Use This Literature Guide (cont.)

Culminating Activity

At the end of this instructional guide is a creative culminating activity that allows students the opportunity to share what they've learned from reading the book. This activity is open ended so that students can push themselves to create their own great works within your language arts classroom.

Comprehension Assessment

The questions in this section require students to think about the book they've read as well as the words that were used in the book. Some questions are tied to quotations from the book to engage students and require them to think about the text as they answer the questions.

Response to Literature

Finally, students are asked to respond to the literature by drawing pictures and writing about the characters and story. A suggested rubric is provided for teacher reference.

Correlation to the Standards

Shell Education is committed to producing educational materials that are research and standards based. As part of this effort, we have correlated all of our products to the academic standards of all 50 states, the District of Columbia, the Department of Defense Dependents Schools, and all Canadian provinces.

Purpose and Intent of Standards

The Every Student Succeeds Act (ESSA) mandates that all states adopt challenging academic standards that help students meet the goal of college and career readiness. While many states already adopted academic standards prior to ESSA, the act continues to hold states accountable for detailed and comprehensive standards. Standards are statements that describe the criteria necessary for students to meet specific academic goals. They define the knowledge, skills, and content students should acquire at each level. State standards are used in the development of our products, so educators can be assured they meet state academic requirements.

How to Find Standards Correlations

To print a customized correlation report of this product for your state, visit our website at **www.teachercreated materials.com/administrators/correlations/** and follow the online directions. If you require assistance in printing correlation reports, please contact our Customer Service Department at 1-877-777-3450.

correlation to the standards (cont.)

standards correlation chart

The lessons in this book were written to support today's college and career readiness standards. The following chart indicates which lessons address each standard.

College and Career Readiness Anchor Standard	Section
Read closely to determine what the text says explicitly and to make logical inferences from it; cite specific textual evidence when writing or speaking to support conclusions drawn from the text.	Vocabulary Sections 3, 5; Guided Close Reading Sections 1–5; Making Connections Section 1, Analyzing the Literature Sections 1–5; Language Learning Sections 2–4; Story Elements Section 2
Determine central ideas or themes of a text and analyze their development; summarize the key supporting details and ideas.	Analyzing the Literature Sections 1–5; Story Elements Sections 1–2; Post-Reading Activities
Analyze how and why individuals, events, or ideas develop and interact over the course of a text.	Guided Close Reading Sections 1–5; Analyzing the Literature Sections 1–5; Story Elements Sections 1–5; Culminating Activity
Interpret words and phrases as they are used in a text, including determining technical, connotative, and figurative meanings, and analyze how specific word choices shape meaning or tone.	Vocabulary Sections 1–5; Language Learning Sections 1, 3, 5
Read and comprehend complex literary and informational texts independently and proficiently.	Entire Unit
Write arguments to support claims in an analysis of substantive topics or texts using valid reasoning and relevant and sufficient evidence.	Reader Response Sections 2, 4
Write informative/explanatory texts to examine and convey complex ideas and information clearly and accurately through the effective selection, organization, and analysis of content.	Reader Response Section 3
Write narratives to develop real or imagined experiences or events using effective technique, well-chosen details and well-structured event sequences.	Reader Response Sections 1, 5

correlation to the standards (cont.)

standards correlation chart (cont.)

College and Career Readiness Anchor Standard	Section
Demonstrate command of the conventions of standard English grammar and usage when writing or speaking.	Language Learning Sections 1–4; Reader Response Sections 1–5
Demonstrate command of the conventions of standard English capitalization, punctuation, and spelling when writing.	Language Learning Section 2; Reader Repsonse Sections 1–5
Determine or clarify the meaning of unknown and multiple-meaning words and phrases by using context clues, analyzing meaningful word parts, and consulting general and specialized reference materials, as appropriate.	Vocabulary Sections 1–5; Language Learning Section 5

TESOL and WIDA Standards

The lessons in this book promote English language development for English language learners. The following TESOL and WIDA English Language Development Standards are addressed through the activities in this book:

- **Standard 1:** English language learners communicate for social and instructional purposes within the school setting.

- **Standard 2:** English language learners communicate information, ideas and concepts necessary for academic success in the content area of language arts.

About the Author—Matt de la Peña

Matt de la Peña grew up in San Diego, California. Little is known about his early life; however, he went to the University of the Pacific on a basketball scholarship and received his bachelor's degree. He went on to receive his master's of fine arts in creative writing at San Diego State University.

Prior to writing *Last Stop on Market Street*, de la Peña was mostly known for his novels. His first novel, *Ball Don't Lie*, was published in 2005. It instantly received recognition as an American Library Association Young Adult Library Services Association (ALA YALSA) Best Book for Young Adults and an ALA YALSA Quick Pick for Reluctant Readers. The novel was made into a movie in 2011.

Mexican WhiteBoy (2008) and *We Were Here* (2009) were also named ALA YALSA Best Book for Young Adults and received other awards as well. His other novels include *I Will Save You* (2010), *The Living* (2013), and *The Hunted* (2015). In addition to his novels, he has also published two books in Scholastic's *Infinity Ring Series*—*Curse of the Ancients* (book five in the series) published in 2013, and *Eternity* (book eight in the series) was published in 2014. De la Peña has also had a number of short stories and essays published.

His first picture book, *A Nation's Hope: The Story of Boxing Legend Joe Louis*, was published in 2011. *Last Stop on Market Street* is only his second picture book; it won the Newbery Award in 2016 and was named a Caldecott Honor Book the same year. In addition to being on *The New York Times Best Seller List*, the book has also been featured on many other best children's literature book lists.

De la Peña lives in Brooklyn where he teaches creative writing at New York University.

Possible Texts for Text Comparisons

Last Stop on Market Street can be compared to other books about relationships with grandmothers or the city. One book that combines both of these ideas is *Abuela* by Arthur Dorros. It is a beautifully illustrated book that tells the story of a girl and her *abuela* (grandmother) riding a bus. While on the trip, the girl wonders what it would be like if she could fly. The girl and her grandmother are swept out of the bus and go on a sightseeing trip of New York City from above. The parallels to as well as the differences from *Last Stop on Market Street* are clear, making it an excellent book for a text comparison.

Book Summary of *Last Stop on Market Street*

Each week after church, Nana and CJ volunteer at the soup kitchen. But this week, CJ doesn't want to go. His friends don't have to go, and it is raining.

On their bus trip across town, CJ sees everything wrong with the world. But Nana sees the world in a different way. She sees beauty. Through CJ's questions, Nana describes the beauty she sees in life, in the city, and in the people they meet along the way.

By the time Nana and CJ get to the last stop on Market Street, CJ begins to realize that Nana sees beauty everywhere she looks. He still does not see it, though. He still sees the dirt and broken streetlamps around him. When CJ sees the familiar faces at the soup kitchen, he finally realizes that he is glad he came ... and Nana is, too!

How to Read the Book

Each section of this instructional guide contains lessons and activities to help students gain an understanding of the story.

- Section 1: Whole Book
- Section 2: Meet Nana and CJ
- Section 3: The Setting
- Section 4: Meet the Bus Riders
- Section 5: Wonderful Wording

Cross-Curricular Connection

This book can be used within a character education unit on thankfulness, having a good outlook on life, and positive thinking.

Possible Texts for Text Sets

- Breece, Hannah. 2014. *An Everyday Kind of Beautiful*. CreateSpace Independent Publishing Platform.
- Dubuc, Marianne. 2015. *The Bus Ride*. Toronto: Kids Can Press.
- Spinelli, Eileen. 2015. *Thankful*. Grand Rapids: Zonderkidz.
- Viorst, Judith. 1987. *Alexander and the Terrible, Horrible, No Good, Very Bad Day*. New York: Atheneum Books for Young Readers.

or

- Huebner, Dawn. 2006. *What to Do When You Grumble Too Much: A Kid's Guide to Overcoming Negativity*. Washington D.C.: Magination Press.
- King, Bill. 2013. *Stinkin' Thinkin' Stinks: A Kid's Guide to the Lighter Side of Life*. Alpine: Bryce Cullen Publishing.

Pre-Reading Theme Thoughts

Directions: Draw a picture of a happy face or a sad face. Your face should show how you feel about each statement. Then, use words to say what you think about each statement.

Statement	How Do You Feel? 😊 ☹️	Why Do You Feel This Way?
It is interesting to meet new people.		
People see things in different ways.		
There is beauty in a dirty city.		
We can learn things from other people.		

Teacher Plans

Vocabulary Overview

Key words and phrases from this section are provided below with definitions and sentences about how the words are used in the story. Introduce and discuss these important vocabulary words with students. If you think these words or other words in the story warrant more time devoted to them, there are suggestions in the introduction for other vocabulary activities (page 5).

Word	Definition	Sentence about Text
patter	strike repeatedly	CJ and Nana see the rain **patter** on the car window.
creaked	made a squeaking sound	The bus **creaks** to a stop.
lurched	made a sudden movement forward	The bus **lurches** forward.
fact	true piece of information	The blind man says it is a **fact** that some people watch the world with their ears.
fine	very good or nice	Nana wears **fine** perfume.
swirled	passed in a whirling motion	The sunset colors **swirl**.
surrounded	enclosed on all sides	CJ feels **surrounded** by dirt.
familiar	frequently seen or experienced	CJ spots **familiar** faces.

Vocabulary Activity

Directions: Write the vocabulary word that best matches the clue.

Words from the Story

patter	creaked	fact	familiar	swirled

1. This is the sound an old floor might have made.

2. This is the way the water moved in the toilet.

3. This is the sound little feet make when they run.

4. This is something that is true.

5. This describes something you are used to.

Teacher Plans

Analyzing the Literature

Provided below are discussion questions you can use in small groups, with the whole class, or for written assignments. Each question is written at two levels so that you can choose the right question for each group of students. For each question, a few key points are provided for your reference as you discuss the book with students.

Story Element	Level 1	Level 2	Key Discussion Points
Plot	Who is telling the story? How do you know?	How does having a narrator tell the story help contrast Nana's and CJ's opposing views of the world?	A narrator is telling the story. The narrator tells what each of the characters says. The pronoun *I* is not used in the book, which would show that the story is told from the point of view of one of the characters. If either Nana or CJ were telling the story, their viewpoints might be more one-sided. Having a narrator tell the story balances Nana's and CJ's opposing views of the world.
Plot	Why does CJ ask why they don't have a car?	How does Nana respond to CJ when he asks why they don't have a car?	CJ sees his friend drive off in a car. Nana responds that they don't need a car because they have a bus that breathes fire and Mr. Dennis, the bus driver, who always has a trick for CJ.
Character	Compare the first sentence CJ says in the book to the last sentence he says. Has CJ changed?	Describe how CJ has changed in the book.	The first sentence of the book is, "How come we gotta wait for the bus in all this wet?" At the beginning of the book, CJ complains about everything. At the end, CJ is happy he has come with Nana to work at the soup kitchen. You can tell because he says, "I'm glad we came."
Setting	Describe the setting at the beginning, middle, and end of the story.	How does changing the setting help the author tell his story?	At the beginning of the story, CJ and Nana are outside a church and waiting at the bus stop. Then, CJ and Nana get on the bus. When they get off the bus, they walk to the soup kitchen. The change in setting allows for Nana and CJ to see many different things in the city and to meet many different people.

Name _____

Reader Response

Think

In *Last Stop on Market Street*, Nana and CJ have the same routine after church. Think about something you do routinely.

Narrative Writing Prompt

Write about a routine you or your family has. Tell about what you do and when you do it.

_____
- -
_____

_____
- -
_____

_____
- -
_____

_____
- -
_____

_____
- -
_____

Name _____

Guided close Reading

Closely reread from when Nana and CJ get off the bus to the end of the story.

Directions: Think about these questions. In the space below, write ideas or draw pictures as you think. Be ready to share your answers.

---

❶ What does CJ see in the sky above the soup kitchen?

---

❷ Describe what CJ sees just after he wonders how Nana can find so much beauty.

---

❸ What evidence is there that tells why CJ is glad they came?

Making connections—Thirsty Plants

Directions: Nana asks CJ if he can see a big tree drinking water through a straw. Do plants really drink through straws? Use celery and food coloring to find out.

Materials

- six drops of food coloring
- one stalk of celery
- a glass of water

Instructions

Place six drops of food coloring into a glass of water. Place a stalk of celery in the cup. Wait for at least six hours. Draw a picture of your observations. Then, answer the question below.

Think about what you observed with the celery. Why do you think Nana says the tree is drinking through a straw?

_____

- -

_____

- -

_____

- -

_____

Name _____

Language Learning—Verbs

Directions: Verbs are words that show action. Write verbs in the chart below that show actions of each character.

Character	Verbs		
Nana	laughed	hummed	knitted
CJ			
the blind man			
the bus			
the rain			

© Shell Education

Story Elements—Setting

Directions: The setting of the story changes. Draw pictures of each setting.

outside the church	at the bus stop
on the bus	in the soup kitchen

Name _____

Story Elements—Plot

Directions: Cut apart the cards below. Glue them on another piece of paper in the order of the story.

CJ and Nana meet interesting people.	CJ and Nana walk to the soup kitchen.
CJ and Nana walk to the bus stop.	CJ and Nana help at the soup kitchen.
CJ and Nana get off the bus.	CJ and Nana come out of church.
CJ and Nana get on the bus.	

© Shell Education

Vocabulary Overview

Key words and phrases from this section are provided below with definitions and sentences about how the words are used in the story. Introduce and discuss these important vocabulary words with students. If you think these words or other words in the story warrant more time devoted to them, there are suggestions in the introduction for other vocabulary activities (page 5).

Word	Definition	Sentence about Text
ducked	moved quickly to avoid	CJ **ducks** under Nana's umbrella.
deep	located far inside	Nana has a **deep** laugh.
knit	make a piece of clothing from yarn or thread by using long needles	Nana **knits** while she is on the bus.
rhythm	flow of sound in music having a regular pattern	The **rhythm** of the music affects CJ.
glanced	looked at quickly	Nana **glances** at CJ's coin.
witness	see something happen	Nana wants CJ to be a **witness** for beauty.
wondered	felt curious about something	CJ **wonders** how his Nana finds beauty everywhere she looks.

Name _____

Vocabulary Activity

Directions: Review the words and definitions. Then, answer the questions.

1. **glanced:** looked at quickly

   Glance around the room. What do you see?

   _____
   _
   _____
   _
   _____

2. **wondered:** felt curious about something

   What is something you have **wondered** about?

   _____
   _
   _____
   _
   _____

3. **witness:** see something happen

   How do you **witness** kindness at your school?

   _____
   _
   _____
   _
   _____

Analyzing the Literature

Provided below are discussion questions you can use in small groups, with the whole class, or for written assignments. Each question is written at two levels so that you can choose the right question for each group of students. For each question, a few key points are provided for your reference as you discuss the book with students.

Story Element	Level 1	Level 2	Key Discussion Points
Character	What evidence is there that Nana is kind?	Describe Nana's character.	Nana is a kind person. She smiles and says good afternoon to everyone on the bus. Nana encourages CJ to put his coin in the guitar player's hat to thank him for the song. Nana takes CJ to work at the soup kitchen each week.
Setting	What is the setting on the first page of the book? What is the setting on the last page of the book?	Think about the setting at the very beginning and ending of the book. What do these two settings tell about Nana?	At the beginning of the book, Nana and CJ have just come out of church. At the end of the book, Nana and CJ are working at a soup kitchen. These two settings show these are important places to Nana. The text also indicates that Nana and CJ go to these two places every week, also showing their importance to her.
Character	Does CJ want to work at the soup kitchen? How do you know?	The author states that CJ feels sorry for himself. What happens to show that CJ is feeling sorry for himself?	The text says, "CJ stared out the window [of the bus] feeling sorry for himself." CJ keeps asking Nana questions about everything. He also wonders why his friends don't have to go anywhere.
Plot	How does CJ change from the beginning of the story to the end of the story?	What happens in the story to change CJ's attitude?	At the beginning of the story, CJ feels sorry for himself and wonders why he has to go work at the soup kitchen. Throughout the story, CJ listens to Nana put a positive spin on everything he questions. At the end of the story, once he sees the familiar faces, he is glad he comes to the soup kitchen to work.

Name _____

Reader Response

Think

In *Last Stop on Market Street*, Nana and CJ see the same things in different ways. CJ describes things exactly as he sees them. Nana creates beauty out of what she sees. Think about which character's view you like more.

Opinion Writing Prompt

Write your opinion about which character's view you like more. Give at least two reasons for your answer.

_____

_ _ _ _ _ _ _ _ _ _ _ _ _ _ _ _ _ _

_____

_ _ _ _ _ _ _ _ _ _ _ _ _ _ _ _ _ _

_____

_ _ _ _ _ _ _ _ _ _ _ _ _ _ _ _ _ _

_____

_ _ _ _ _ _ _ _ _ _ _ _ _ _ _ _ _ _

_____

_ _ _ _ _ _ _ _ _ _ _ _ _ _ _ _ _ _

_____

Guided close Reading

Closely reread the pages where CJ asks why they don't have a car and Nana gives her response.

Directions: Think about these questions. In the space below, write ideas or draw pictures as you think. Be ready to share your answers.

---

❶ What event happens just before CJ asks Nana why they don't have a car?

---

❷ How does Nana describe the bus?

---

❸ How does the author describe the sounds the bus makes?

Name _____

Making connections—Family

Directions: CJ calls his grandmother *Nana*. Different people call their family members by different names. Complete the chart by writing the names you use for people in your family. Compare the names you use with the names your classmates use.

Person	Name You Call Him/Her
mom(s)	
dad(s)	
grandmother(s)	
grandfather(s)	
aunt(s)	
uncle(s)	

Language Learning—Questions

Directions: CJ asks Nana a lot of questions throughout the story. Questions end with a question mark. Look through the story and write four questions CJ asks. Circle the question mark at the end of each of your sentences.

1. _____

_____

_____

2. _____

_____

_____

3. _____

_____

_____

4. _____

_____

_____

Name _____

Story Elements—character

Directions: The words below describe Nana. Write a sentence from the book to support each word that describes Nana.

Word	Supporting Sentence
polite	
positive	
helpful	

Story Elements—Plot

Directions: Nana always has great answers to CJ's questions. Write your own question CJ could ask Nana. Write a positive and creative answer Nana might give. Draw a picture of what CJ is looking at when he asks the question.

CJ: _____
_____
_____

Nana: _____
_____
_____

Vocabulary Overview

Key words and phrases from this section are provided below with definitions and sentences about how the words are used in the story. Introduce and discuss these important vocabulary words with students. If you think these words or other words in the story warrant more time devoted to them, there are suggestions in the introduction for other vocabulary activities (page 5).

Word	Definition	Sentence about Text
freckled	sprinkled or marked	The rain **freckles** CJ's shirt.
breathes	to send out by exhaling	Nana describes the bus as a bus that **breathes** fire.
crumbling	falling apart into smaller pieces	The sidewalks are **crumbling**.
graffiti-tagged	unlawful writing on public spaces, usually with spray paint	The windows are **graffiti-tagged**.
boarded-up	windows or doors that have wooden boards covering them	CJ passes **boarded-up** stores.
arcing	moving in a curving path	A rainbow **arches** in the sky.
soup kitchen	place that gives food to poor people	CJ and Nana volunteer at a **soup kitchen**.

Vocabulary Activity

Directions: Each of these sentences uses at least one vocabulary word from the book. Cut apart these sentence strips. Put the sentences in order. Use the story to help you.

The bus **breathes** fire.

Nana and CJ walk past **graffiti-tagged** windows and **boarded-up** stores.

A rainbow is **arcing** in the sky.

The rain **freckled** CJ's shirt.

CJ sees **crumbling** sidewalks and broken-down doors.

Nana and CJ work in the **soup kitchen**.

Teacher Plans

Analyzing the Literature

Provided below are discussion questions you can use in small groups, with the whole class, or for written assignments. Each question is written at two levels so that you can choose the right question for each group of students. For each question, a few key points are provided for your reference as you discuss the book with students.

Story Element	Level 1	Level 2	Key Discussion Points
Setting	How does the author describe the bus?	How do the illustrations support why Nana says the bus breathes fire?	Nana says the bus breathes fire. The illustrations show a poster of a dragon breathing fire on the side of the bus.
Character	How does Nana see the world? How does CJ see the world?	What can readers learn from the characters' different views?	In the story, CJ sees how beautiful the world looks to Nana in contrast to how he sees the world. Readers can learn that there are many ways to look at the world. Some people see the dirt in the world and some people see the beauty.
Character	Who are the main characters? Who are the secondary characters?	Which secondary character do Nana and CJ interact with the most?	Nana and CJ are the main characters that are in every scene. The secondary characters include all the people they see and talk about in the city and on the bus. CJ and Nana interact with the blind man the most. The blind man tells them about how he uses his senses to see the world. It is also the blind man who encourages CJ to shut his eyes to feel the rhythm and magic of the music.
Setting	How is the setting of rain important to the rainbow at the end of the story?	What does the rainbow at the end of the story symbolize?	There would not be a rainbow if it had not been raining in the story. The rainbow at the end of the story symbolizes the beauty that Nana sees in contrast to the dirty city that CJ sees.

Reader Response

Think

The weather is rainy in *Last Stop on Market Street*. Think about what the sky and the earth look like when it rains.

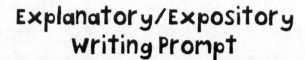

Explanatory/Expository Writing Prompt

Write about rainy weather. Include at least two facts you know about the rain.

_____

_____

_____

_____

_____

_____

_____

_____

_____

_____

_____

Name _____

Guided close Reading

Closely reread the first six pages where the rainy day is described.

Directions: Think about these questions. In the space below, write ideas or draw pictures as you think. Be ready to share your answers.

❶ What does the author mean when he says the rain freckled CJ's shirt?

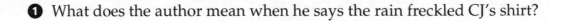

❷ What words does Nana use to describe the tree being watered by the rain?

❸ How do the illustrations support the description of rain in the text?

Making connections—Rainbows

Directions: Use crayons or watercolor paints to fill in the rainbow. You can remember the order of the colors of a rainbow by using the name, Roy G. Biv.

R o y	**G**.	**B** i v
e r e	r	I n v
d a l	e	n d i
n l	e	u e o
g o	n	e i l
e w		g g e
		o o t

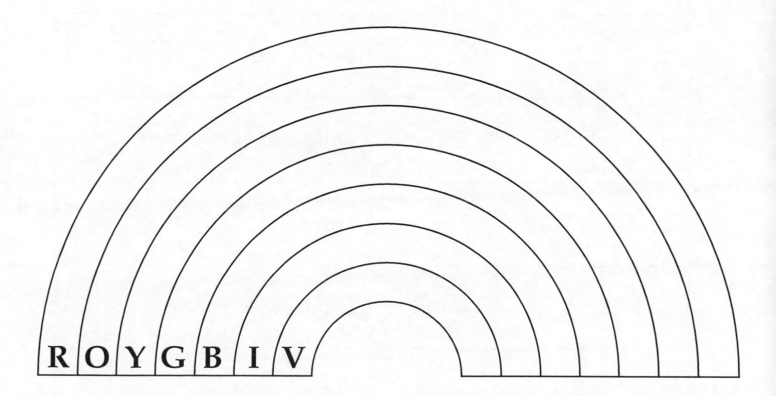

R O Y G B I V

Name _____

Language Learning—
Descriptive Language

Directions: The author uses interesting words to describe the setting. Reread the end of the book to find the words used to describe what CJ sees as he walks from the bus stop.

Descriptive Word(s)	What CJ Sees
1.	sidewalks
2.	doors
3.	windows
4.	stores
5.	rainbow
6.	streetlamps
7.	shadows

Story Elements—Plot

Directions: Draw a picture of each setting below. Then, cut apart the cards. Glue them on another piece of paper in the order CJ saw them.

bus stop	soup kitchen
rainbow	church
crumbling sidewalks	bus

Name _____

Story Elements—Setting

Directions: Listen to your teacher read the paragraph below. Then, draw a picture of the bus.

> A bus is a vehicle that gets people from place to place. In *Last Stop on Market Street*, it is so much more! It becomes part of the setting. Reread the page where the bus pulls up to the bus stop. Draw a picture of the bus. Try to illustrate the way the author describes the bus.

Vocabulary Overview

Key words and phrases from this section are provided below with definitions and sentences about how the words are used in the story. Introduce and discuss these important vocabulary words with students. If you think these words or other words in the story warrant more time devoted to them, there are suggestions in the introduction for other vocabulary activities (page 5).

Word	Definition	Sentence about Text
palm	underside of the hand	The bus driver puts a coin in CJ's **palm**.
tuning	adjusting in musical pitch	The man is **tuning** his guitar.
curlers	devices on which hair is wound for curling	The old woman has **curlers** in her hair.
sniffing	smelling	The blind man **sniffs** Nana's perfume.
perfume	pleasant smelling liquid placed on the body	Nana wears **perfume**.
plucking	playing an instrument by pulling strings with fingers or a pick	The man **plucks** the strings of the guitar to play a song.
whispered	spoken very softly	The man **whispers** to Nana.

Name _____

Vocabulary Activity

Directions: Choose at least four words from the story. Draw pictures that show what these words mean. Label the pictures.

Analyzing the Literature

Provided below are discussion questions you can use in small groups, with the whole class, or for written assignments. Each question is written at two levels so that you can choose the right question for each group of students. For each question, a few key points are provided for your reference as you discuss the book with students.

Story Element	Level 1	Level 2	Key Discussion Points
Plot	Who is on the bus when Nana and CJ get on?	In what ways do Nana and CJ interact with the people on the bus?	The guitar man, the lady with the butterflies in a jar, and Bobo are already on the bus when Nana and CJ get on. First, a blind man climbs aboard. Next, two older boys get on. Nana and CJ interact with the blind man and discuss the two older boys.
Character	How did the blind man show that he uses his sense of smell?	Why does the blind man comment on Nana's perfume?	Nana comments that blind people watch the world with their ears, and the blind man adds that they use their noses, too. He comments on Nana's perfume to show how he uses his sense of smell.
Plot	How does Nana respond to CJ when he wants a music player?	When the two older boys get on the bus, CJ says he "wishes he has one of those." How do the illustrations and the text show what CJ wants?	The illustrations show two older boys listening to a music player. When CJ tells Nana that he wants one of those, she replies that she doesn't know why he would want a music player when he can listen to live music from the guitar player.
Plot	Why does CJ close his eyes?	What happens when CJ closes his eyes?	CJ closes his eyes because the blind man tells CJ that he closes his eyes to feel the magic of music. When CJ closes his eyes, he experiences the music by visualizing what he thinks it looks like.

Name _____

Reader Response

Think

Nana and CJ see many interesting people while they are on the bus. Think about which of these people you would most like to meet.

Opinion Writing Prompt

Write your opinion about which character from the bus you would most like to meet. Include at least two reasons for your opinion.

Guided Close Reading

Closely reread the pages where Nana and CJ talk to the blind man.

Directions: Think about these questions. In the space below, write ideas or draw pictures as you think. Be ready to share your answers.

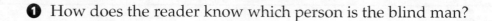

❶ How does the reader know which person is the blind man?

❷ What does the blind man do to show that he sees with his nose?

❸ Why does Nana squeeze the blind man's hand and laugh?

Name _____

Making connections—Using Senses

Directions: Go outside and sit down on a bench or on the ground. Close your eyes and use your other senses to help you experience the world around you. Write about what you experience.

_____

- -

_____

_____

- -

_____

_____

- -

_____

_____

- -

_____

_____

- -

_____

_____

- -

_____

Language Learning—Adjectives

Directions: Adjectives are describing words. Listed below are adjectives used in the book. Reread the story to find and list the nouns they describe.

Adjective	Noun	Adjective + Noun
1. brand-new	hat	brand-new hat
2. spotted		
3. fine		
4. older		

Name _____

Story Elements—Character

Directions: Think about the two characters below. Write what Nana wanted CJ to learn from each character.

blind man with the spotted dog

the man with the guitar

Name _____

Story Elements—Character

Directions: Choose one of the characters on the bus. Draw a picture of him or her in the space below. Write four words to describe the character.

1. _____   2. _____

3. _____   4. _____

Teacher Plans

Vocabulary Overview

Key words and phrases from this section are provided below with definitions and sentences about how the words are used in the story. Introduce and discuss these important vocabulary words with students. If you think these words or other words in the story warrant more time devoted to them, there are suggestions in the introduction for other vocabulary activities (page 5).

Word	Definition	Sentence about Text
freedom	state or quality of being free	The air smells like **freedom**.
wet	having a lot of water	CJ and Nana use an umbrella in the **wet**.
pool	to puddle	The water **pools** on the flower petals.
sighed	made a sound like a long breath	The bus **sighs** when it stops.
sagged	hung down or drooped	The bus **sags** when it stops.
slicing	cutting through	The hawks are **slicing** through the sky.
magic	something that charms	Music gives CJ a feeling of **magic**.
grew	expanded	CJ's chest **grows** full when he hears the music.
lost	filled with strong emotion	CJ becomes **lost** in the sound of the music.

Vocabulary Activity

Directions: Complete each sentence below. Use the words listed below.

Words from the Story

growls	slicing	sighs	wet
sags	magic	lost	pool

_____

_ _ _ _ _ _ _ _ _

1. In all the _____, CJ sees water

_ _ _ _ _ _ _ _ _

_____ on the flower petals.

_____

_ _ _ _ _ _ _ _ _

2. When it stops, the bus _____ and

_ _ _ _ _ _ _

_____.

_____

_ _ _ _ _ _ _ _

3. The _____ of the music makes CJ get

_ _ _ _ _ _

_____.

_____

_ _ _ _ _ _ _ _

4. He sees hawks _____ through the sky.

Teacher Plans

Analyzing the Literature

Provided below are discussion questions you can use in small groups, with the whole class, or for written assignments. Each question is written at two levels so that you can choose the right question for each group of students. For each question, a few key points are provided for your reference as you discuss the book with students.

Story Element	Level 1	Level 2	Key Discussion Points
Setting	What words does the author use to describe the rain?	How can the reader tell how hard it is raining from the illustrations and the words used?	The author uses words such as *dripped*, *patter*, and *pooled* to describe the rain and the effects of the rain. There are puddles on the ground and raindrops in the sky in the illustrations, and Nana and CJ have to use an umbrella.
Plot	Why does CJ close his eyes to listen to the music?	How does closing his eyes enhance CJ's experience of the music?	The blind man says he closes his eyes so he can feel the magic of music. When the blind man first gets on the bus, Nana tells CJ that some people watch the world with their ears. By closing their eyes, the blind man, Nana, and CJ are using only their ears to listen to the music.
Plot	What verbs are used in the description of CJ's experience while he listens to the music?	What hints from the text and illustrations tell the reader that CJ enjoys his music experience?	CJ sees sunset colors swirling, crashing waves, hawks slicing through the sky, and butterflies dancing. CJ's chest grows full, and he gets lost in the music. The sound gives him the feeling of magic. The illustration also shows a smile on CJ's face. CJ also drops his coin in the guitar man's hat when he opens his eyes.
Character	What words does the author use to describe how CJ and Nana see the city when they get off the bus?	Describe how CJ sees the city after he realizes that Nana always sees beauty.	CJ sees crumbling sidewalks, broken-down doors, graffiti-tagged windows, and boarded-up stores. Even after he realizes that Nana sees beauty everywhere she looks, CJ still sees broken streetlamps and stray-cat shadows.

Reader Response

Think

CJ has a wonderful experience when he listens to the rhythm of the guitar player's music. Think about how you feel when you hear music.

Narrative Writing Prompt

Write a description of how you feel when you hear music. Try to include some descriptive wording to explain how you feel.

_____

- -

_____

- -

_____

- -

_____

- -

_____

- -

_____

- -

_____

Name _____

Guided close Reading

Closely reread the pages when the guitar man plays his song.

Directions: Think about these questions. In the space below, write ideas or draw pictures as you think. Be ready to share your answers.

❶ What do the bus riders do to feel the magic of the music?

❷ Describe what happens when CJ experiences the magic of music.

❸ How do the bus riders show the guitar man they liked his song?

Making connections—Music

Directions: Close your eyes while listening to some music. Then, open your eyes and draw what you experienced. Share your picture with a friend.

Language Learning—
Multiple Meaning Words

Directions: Some words have more than one meaning. Look at the sentences from the book. Circle the correct meaning of each bold word.

Sentence from the Story	Meaning 1	Meaning 2
"He **ducked** under his nana's umbrella."	web-footed bird	to lower quickly
"He watched water **pool** on flower petals."	deep area of water for swimming	to puddle
"He pulled a coin from behind CJ's ear, placed it in his **palm**."	underside of the hand	tropical plant with fan-shaped leaves
"Nana laughed her **deep** laugh and pushed CJ along."	dark in color	having a low, loud sound
"He watched cars **zip** by on either side."	move or act quickly	pull up a zipper

Story Elements—Character

Directions: Nana and CJ were looking at the same things in different ways. Read the negative view CJ sees. Then, write the positive view that Nana sees.

Negative	Positive
1. "Nana, how come we don't got a car?"	
2. "Miguel and Colby never have to go nowhere."	
3. "Sure wish I had one of those [music players]."	
4. "How come it's always so dirty over here?"	

Name _____

Story Elements—Setting

Directions: Draw a picture of the city as CJ sees it and as Nana sees it. Use the text to help you.

How CJ sees the city

How Nana sees the city

Post-Reading Theme Thoughts

Directions: Choose a main character from *Last Stop on Market Street*. Pretend you are that character. Draw a picture of a happy face or a sad face to show how the character would feel about each statement. Then, use words to explain your picture.

Character I Chose: _____

Statement	How Do You Feel? ☺ ☹	Explain Your Answer
It is interesting to meet new people.		
People see things in different ways.		
There is beauty in a dirty city.		
We can learn things from other people.		

Culminating Activity: Seeing Beauty

Directions: Nana was able to find beauty in everything she saw and everyone she met on the bus trip to the soup kitchen. This culminating activity gives students the opportunity to do the same. Through an illustration, an interview, and a brief writing assignment, students will seek to find beauty in all people.

Begin by having students select a person on whom to focus such as the custodian, the librarian, or even an older student. It can also be someone they know from another setting such as home, sports, or church. Assist students, as needed, by brainstorming people they might want to consider.

Character Illustration—Draw students' attention to the style the illustrator uses throughout the book. Discuss the simplistic shapes and bold colors. On page 61, have students design a character for *Last Stop on Market Street* based on the person they have chosen. Students can use any medium you provide them; however, one way to get students to mimic the book's style is to have students cut out shapes from construction paper.

Interview—Have students write two questions to ask during a brief interview. Discuss the types of questions that will help them get to know the person better, rather than surface-level questions. As a class, create a list of possible questions that students can draw upon if they cannot think of any by themselves. Provide students time to conduct their interviews either during the school day or as part of a homework assignment. Have students record the answers on page 62.

Character Lesson—Using the *Character Lesson* (page 63), students combine the interview and the character drawing to show the beauty that was found in the person interviewed. Students illustrate their character doing something they learned about during the interview and then write two to three sentences. Encourage students to use descriptive and creative wording as they write.

Name _____

Culminating Activity: Seeing Beauty (cont.)

Character Illustration

Directions: Think about a person you know who might make a good character in *Last Stop on Market Street*. Then, draw that person in the same style as the art in the book.

culminating Activity: Seeing Beauty (cont.)

character Interview

Directions: Think about the person you chose to draw. Write two questions you would like to ask the person. Then, interview the person and write the answers below.

_____

Question 1: _____

_____

_____

_____

Answer: _____

_____

_____

_____

Question 2: _____

_____

_____

_____

Answer: _____

_____

_____

culminating Activity: Seeing Beauty (cont.)

character Lesson

Directions: Think about the person you interviewed and the character drawing you made. Draw a picture of your character. Describe what your character is doing.

_____

- - - - - - - - - - - - - - - - - - - -

_____

- - - - - - - - - - - - - - - - - - - -

_____

- - - - - - - - - - - - - - - - - - - -

_____

- - - - - - - - - - - - - - - - - - - -

_____

Name _____

Comprehension Assessment

Directions: Fill in the bubble for the best response to each question.

Section 1: Story Overview

1. Which sentence best describes how Nana sees the world?

    (A) Nana meets many people.

    (B) Nana finds beauty everywhere she looks.

    (C) Nana likes to close her eyes to listen to music.

    (D) Nana sees a dirty city that is falling apart.

Section 2: Meet Nana and CJ

2. Why does Nana tell CJ, "I feel sorry for those boys."

    (A) Miguel and Colby do not get to meet interesting people.

    (B) Miguel and Colby do not get to ride the bus.

    (C) Miguel and Colby never have to go anywhere.

    (D) Miguel and Colby do not get to play with CJ.

Section 3: The Setting

3. Why is CJ glad he came once he gets to the soup kitchen?

    (A) He wants to ride the bus.

    (B) He sees familiar faces.

    (C) He sees the rainbow over the soup kitchen.

    (D) He wants to go home like Miguel and Colby.

comprehension Assessment (cont.)

Section 4: Meet the Bus Riders

4. Describe what Nana wants CJ to learn from the blind man.

_____

- - - - - - - - - - - - - - - - - -

_____

_____

- - - - - - - - - - - - - - - - - -

_____

_____

- - - - - - - - - - - - - - - - - -

Section 5: Wonderful Wording

5. Which of the following is not a reason Nana says, "Sometimes when you're surrounded by dirt, CJ, you're a better witness for what's beautiful"?

(A) Nana sees beauty everywhere she looks.

(B) She wants CJ to see the beauty in things.

(C) She sees the rainbow over the soup kitchen.

(D) CJ sees beauty everywhere he looks.

Name _____

Response to Literature: Creating Beauty

Directions: Think of something you see every day that is dirty or that does not look very nice. Draw a picture of it in the space below. Then, answer the questions on the next page.

Response to Literature: Creating Beauty (cont.)

Directions: Use your drawing on page 66 to help you answer the questions.

1. Describe what you drew in your picture. Where do you see it? Why is it not very nice to look at?

_____

- - - - - - - - - - - - - - - - - - - -

_____

- - - - - - - - - - - - - - - - - - - -

_____

2. Think about your drawing the way Nana would. Describe it again as you look for the beauty in it.

_____

- - - - - - - - - - - - - - - - - - - -

_____

- - - - - - - - - - - - - - - - - - - -

_____

3. Is it easy to see the beauty in things that might not look nice? Why?

_____

- - - - - - - - - - - - - - - - - - - -

_____

- - - - - - - - - - - - - - - - - - - -

_____

Name _____

Response to Literature Rubric

Directions: Use this rubric to evaluate student responses.

Great Job	Good Work	Keep Trying
☐ You answered all three questions completely. You included many details.	☐ You answered all three questions.	☐ You did not answer all three questions.
☐ Your handwriting is very neat. There are no spelling errors.	☐ Your handwriting can be neater. There are some spelling errors.	☐ Your handwriting is not very neat. There are many spelling errors.
☐ Your picture is neat and fully colored.	☐ Your picture is neat, and some of it is colored.	☐ Your picture is not very neat and/or fully colored.
☐ Creativity is clear in the picture and the writing.	☐ Creativity is clear in either the picture or the writing.	☐ There is not much creativity in either the picture or the writing.

Teacher Comments: _____

_____

_____

_____

Name _____

The responses provided here are just examples of what the students may answer. Many accurate responses are possible for the questions throughout this unit.

Vocabulary Activity—Section 1:
Whole Book (page 15)

1. creaked
2. swirled
3. patter
4. fact
5. familiar

Guided Close Reading—Section 1:
Whole Book (page 18)

1. When CJ gets to the soup kitchen, he sees a rainbow arcing over it. A rainbow is possible because the weather is rainy.
2. CJ looks around again and he still sees broken streetlamps and stray-cat shadows.
3. The text states that CJ says he is glad he came when he sees familiar faces in the window of the soup kitchen.

Language Learning—Section 1:
Whole Book (page 20)

Character	Verbs
Nana	laughed, hummed, knitted
CJ	pushed, skipped, ducked, looked, watched, stared, gave, saw, grew, opened, clapped, dropped, reached, wondered, thought, spotted
the blind man	sniffed, close, clapped
the bus	creaked, sighed, sagged, lurched, stopped
the rain	freckled, dripped, pool, patter

Story Elements—Section 1:
Whole Book (page 22)

1. CJ and Nana come out of church.
2. CJ and Nana walk to the bus stop.
3. CJ and Nana get on the bus.
4. CJ and Nana meet interesting people on the bus.
5. CJ and Nana get off the bus.
6. CJ and Nana walk to the soup kitchen.
7. CJ and Nana help at the soup kitchen.

Guided Close Reading—Section 2:
Whole Book (page 27)

1. CJ sees his friend Colby drive off in a car with his dad.
2. Nana says they have a bus that breathes fire.
3. The author uses the words *creaked* and *sighed* to describe the sounds of the bus.

Story Elements—Section 2:
Meet Nana and CJ (page 30)

polite: "Nana gave everyone a great big smile and a 'good afternoon.'"

positive: Answers will vary but should be any sentence from the book describing how Nana sees things in a positive way, for example, she doesn't worry about the wet, she sees the trees drinking water.

helpful: Nana goes to work in the soup kitchen each week after church.

Vocabulary Activity—Section 3:
The Setting (page 33)

1. The rain **freckled** CJ's shirt.
2. The bus **breathes** fire.
3. CJ sees **crumbling** sidewalks and broken-down doors.
4. Nana and CJ walk passed **graffiti-tagged** windows and **boarded-up** stores.
5. A rainbow is **arcing** in the sky.

6. Nana and CJ work in the **soup kitchen**.

Guided Close Reading—Section 3:
The Setting (page 36)

1. The author means the rain creates wet spots that look like freckles on CJ's shirts.

2. Nana says the tree is drinking through a straw.

3. The illustrations show raindrops falling through the sky. They show puddles forming on the ground. The illustrations also show people carrying umbrellas.

Language Learning—Section 3:
The Setting (page 38)

Descriptive Word(s)	What CJ Sees
1. **crumbling**	sidewalks
2. **broken-down**	doors
3. **graffiti-tagged**	windows
4. **boarded-up**	stores
5. **beautiful**	rainbow
6. **broken**	streetlamps
7. **stray-cat**	shadows

Story Elements—Section 3:
The Setting (page 39)

1. church
2. bus stop
3. bus
4. crumbling sidewalks
5. rainbow
6. soup kitchen

Guided Close Reading—Section 4:
Meet the Bus Riders (page 45)

1. The man is carrying a cane and has a seeing-eye dog. He is also wearing sunglasses.

2. The blind man sniffs the air and comments on Nana's perfume.

3. Nana squeezes the blind man's hand and laughs as a way to acknowledge the kind comment he just made.

Language Learning—Section 4:
Meet the Bus Riders (page 47)

Adjective	Noun	Adjective + Noun
1. brand-new	hat	brand-new had
2. spotted	dog	spotted dog
3. fine	perfume	fine perfume
4. older	boys	older boys

Vocabulary Activity—Section 5:
Wonderful Wording (page 51)

1. In all the **wet**, CJ sees water **pool** on the flower petals.

2. When it stops, the bus **sighs** and **sags**.

3. The **magic** of the music makes CJ get **lost**.

4. He sees hawks **slicing** through the sky.

Guided Close Reading—Section 5:
Wonderful Wording (page 54)

1. The bus riders close their eyes.

2. CJ gets lost in the music and he sees "sunset colors swirling over crashing waves," "a family of hawks slicing through the sky," and "butterflies dancing free."

3. The bus riders clap, and CJ gives the guitar player the coin that Mr. Dennis pulled out from behind his ear.

Language Learning—Section 5:
Wonderful Wording (page 56)
Answers that should be circled:

to lower quickly

to puddle

underside of the hand

having a low, loud sound

move or act quickly

**Story Elements—Section 5:
Wonderful Wording** (page 57)

Negative	Positive
1. "Nana, how come we don't got a car?"	"Boy, what do we need a car for? We got a bus that breathes fire."
2. "Miguel and Colby never have to go nowhere."	"I feel sorry for those boys ... They'll never get to meet Bobo or the Sunglass Man."
3. "Sure wish I had one of those [music players]."	"What for? You got the real live thing sitting across from you."
4. "How come it's always so dirty over here?"	"Sometimes when you're surrounded by dirt, CJ, you're a better witness for what's beautiful."

Comprehension Assessment (page 64)

1. B. Nana finds beauty everywhere she looks.

2. A. Miguel and Colby do not get to meet interesting people.

3. B. He sees familiar faces.

4. Nana wants CJ to learn that even though some people cannot see, they can experience the world in other ways.

5. D. CJ sees beauty everywhere he looks.